LIFE
Lessons

WITH MAX LUCADO

BOOK OF EPHESIANS

WHERE YOU BELONG

MAX LUCADO

Prepared by

THE LIVINGSTONE CORPORATION

NELSON IMPACT
A Division of Thomas Nelson Publishers
Since 1798

Published by Nelson Impact, a Division of Thomas Nelson, Inc., P.O. Box 141000, Nashville, TN, 37214.

Produced with the assistance of the Livingstone Corporation (www.livingstonecorp.com). Project staff include Jake Barton, Joel Bartlett, Andy Culbertson, Mary Horner Collins, and Will Reaves.

Editor: Neil Wilson

Cover Art and Interior Design by Kirk Luttrell of the Livingstone Corporation

Interior Composition by Rachel Hawkins of the Livingstone Corporation

ISBN-13: 978-1-4185-0953-8

LIFE Lessons

WITH MAX LUCADO

CONTENTS

How to Study the Bible   iv

Introduction to the Book of Ephesians   vi

Lesson 1   Where Do You Belong?   1

Lesson 2   The Power of Our Faith   11

Lesson 3   Have Mercy!   21

Lesson 4   Family Ties and Racial Blurs   31

Lesson 5   God Had a Secret?   41

Lesson 6   The Amazing Love of Christ   51

Lesson 7   Body Parts Everywhere   61

Lesson 8   The Power of Words   71

Lesson 9   Choosing to Walk in the Light   81

Lesson 10   Don't Miss the Yield Signs   91

Lesson 11   Being Good Parents, Being Good Bosses   101

Lesson 12   Be a Winner!   111

HOW TO
STUDY THE BIBLE

This is a peculiar book you are holding. Words crafted in another language. Deeds done in a distant era. Events recorded in a far-off land. Counsel offered to a foreign people. This is a peculiar book.

It's surprising that anyone reads it. It's too old. Some of its writings date back five thousand years. It's too bizarre. The book speaks of incredible floods, fires, earthquakes, and people with supernatural abilities. It's too radical. The Bible calls for undying devotion to a carpenter who called himself God's Son.

Logic says this book shouldn't survive. Too old, too bizarre, too radical.

The Bible has been banned, burned, scoffed, and ridiculed. Scholars have mocked it as foolish. Kings have branded it as illegal. A thousand times over, the grave has been dug and the dirge has begun, but somehow the Bible never stays in the grave. Not only has it survived; it has thrived. It is the single most popular book in all of history. It has been the best-selling book in the world for years!

There is no way on earth to explain it. Which perhaps is the only explanation. The answer? The Bible's durability is not found on earth; it is found in heaven. For the millions who have tested its claims and claimed its promises, there is but one answer: the Bible is God's book and God's voice.

As you read it, you would be wise to give some thought to two questions. What is the purpose of the Bible? and How do I study the Bible? Time spent reflecting on these two issues will greatly enhance your Bible study.

What is the purpose of the Bible?

Let the Bible itself answer that question.

Since you were a child you have known the Holy Scriptures which are able to make you wise. And that wisdom leads to salvation through faith in Christ Jesus. (2 Tim. 3:15 NCV)

The purpose of the Bible? Salvation. God's highest passion is to get his children home. His book, the Bible, describes his plan of salvation. The purpose of the Bible is to proclaim God's plan and passion to save his children.

That is the reason this book has endured through the centuries. It dares to tackle the toughest questions about life: Where do I go after I die? Is there a God? What do I do with my fears? The Bible offers answers to these crucial questions. It is the treasure map that leads us to God's highest treasure, eternal life.

But how do we use the Bible? Countless copies of Scripture sit unread on bookshelves and nightstands simply because people don't know how to read it. What can we do to make the Bible real in our lives?

The clearest answer is found in the words of Jesus. He promised:

Ask, and God will give to you. Search, and you will find. Knock, and the door will open for you. (Matt. 7:7 NCV)

The first step in understanding the Bible is asking God to help us. We should read prayerfully. If anyone understands God's Word, it is because of God and not the reader.

But the Helper will teach you everything and will cause you to remember all that I told you. The Helper is the Holy Spirit whom the Father will send in my name. (John 14:26 NCV)

Before reading the Bible, pray. Invite God to speak to you. Don't go to Scripture looking for your idea; go searching for his.

Not only should we read the Bible prayerfully; we should read it carefully. *Search and you will find* is the pledge. The Bible is not a newspaper to be skimmed but rather a mine to be quarried.

Search for it like silver, and hunt for it like hidden treasure. Then you will understand respect for the LORD, and you will find that you know God. (Prov. 2:4–5 NCV)

Any worthy find requires effort. The Bible is no exception. To understand the Bible you don't have to be brilliant, but you must be willing to roll up your sleeves and search.

Be a worker who is not ashamed and who uses the true teaching in the right way. (2 Tim. 2:15 NCV)

Here's a practical point. Study the Bible a bit at a time. Hunger is not satisfied by eating twenty-one meals in one sitting once a week. The body needs a steady diet to remain strong. So does the soul. When God sent food to his people in the wilderness, he didn't provide loaves already made. Instead, he sent them manna in the shape of *"thin flakes like frost . . . on the desert ground"* (Ex. 16:14 NCV).

God gave manna in limited portions. God sends spiritual food the same way. He opens the heavens with just enough nutrients for today's hunger. He provides *"a command here, a command there. A rule here, a rule there. A little lesson here, a little lesson there"* (Isa. 28:10 NCV).

Don't be discouraged if your reading reaps a small harvest. Some days a lesser portion is all that is needed. What is important is to search every day for that day's message. A steady diet of God's Word over a lifetime builds a healthy soul and mind.

A little girl returned from her first day at school. Her mom asked, "Did you learn anything?"

"Apparently not enough," the girl responded, "I have to go back tomorrow and the next day and the next . . ."

Such is the case with learning. And such is the case with Bible study. Understanding comes little by little over a lifetime.

There is a third step in understanding the Bible. After the asking and seeking comes the knocking. After you ask and search, then knock.

Knock, and the door will open for you. (Matt. 7:7 NCV)

To knock is to stand at God's door. To make yourself available. To climb the steps, cross the porch, stand at the doorway, and volunteer. Knocking goes beyond the realm of thinking and into the realm of acting.

To knock is to ask, What can I do? How can I obey? Where can I go?

It's one thing to know what to do. It's another to do it. But for those who do it, those who choose to obey, a special reward awaits them.

The truly happy are those who carefully study God's perfect law that makes people free, and they continue to study it. They do not forget what they heard, but they obey what God's teaching says. Those who do this will be made happy. (James 1:25 NCV)

What a promise. Happiness comes to those who do what they read! It's the same with medicine. If you only read the label but ignore the pills, it won't help. It's the same with food. If you only read the recipe but never cook, you won't be fed. And it's the same with the Bible. If you only read the words but never obey, you'll never know the joy God has promised.

Ask. Search. Knock. Simple, isn't it? Why don't you give it a try? If you do, you'll see why you are holding the most remarkable book in history.

INTRODUCTION TO THE BOOK OF EPHESIANS

I've just witnessed a beautiful wedding. The most beautiful I've ever seen. That says a lot, since I've seen a lot. Ministers see many weddings. It's a perk of the profession.

Is there anything more elegant than a wedding? Candles bathe a chapel in gold. Loving families fill the pews. Groomsmen and bridesmaids descend the aisles with bouquets of newness and rings of promise. What an occasion.

And nothing quite compares with that moment when the bride stands at the top of the aisle. Arm entwined with her father's, she takes those final steps with him and steps toward a new life with her groom.

Ahhh, the glory of a wedding. So to say I just saw the most beautiful one is no small thing. What made these nuptials so unforgettable? The groom. Usually the groom is not the star of the wedding. The fellow is typically upstaged by the girl. But this wedding was made special by the groom. It was enhanced by something he did.

And who he was made what he did even more startling. You see, he's a cowboy: a stocky fellow who went to college on a rodeo scholarship. But the one standing by me was not a macho calf roper, but a pinch-me-I'm-dreaming boy who'd never seen a bride so gorgeous.

He was composed as he walked down the aisle. He was fine as he took his place at the altar.

But when he saw the bride, he wept.

It was the moment he'd dreamed of. It was as if he'd been given life's greatest gift—a bride in all her beauty. By the way, those are the very words Paul uses to describe the church: a bride in all her beauty.

"[Jesus] died so he could give the church to himself like a bride in all her beauty. He died so that the church could be pure and without fault, with no evil or sin or any other wrong thing in it" (Eph. 5:27 NCV).

Ponder that verse. Jesus died for a bride. He died so he could be married. This passage anticipates the day when the groom will see his bride—when Christ will receive his church. Jesus' fondest longing will be fulfilled. His Bride will arrive.

The letter to the Ephesians celebrates the beauty of the church—the Bride of Christ. From our perspective the church isn't so pretty. We see the backbiting, the squabbling, the divisions. Heaven sees that, as well. But heaven sees more. Heaven sees the church as cleansed and made holy by Christ.

Heaven sees the church ascending to heaven. Heaven sees the Bride wearing the spotless gown of Jesus Christ.

It's enough to make one weep.

LESSON ONE

WHERE DO YOU BELONG?

MAX LUCADO

REFLECTION

Paul opens his letter with a glorious anthem of praise for all the blessings we have "in Christ." One blessing is that we belong to God's family—a community of faith. Think of a time when you felt a true sense of belonging to a community or group of people. Consider the atmosphere, circumstances, and purpose of the group. What did it feel like to belong?

SITUATION

The apostle Paul had much invested in the church in Ephesus. For three years Paul lived and worked there, providing a strong foundation for the church. In all likelihood, this letter was intended for a region made up of several churches. Paul sent the manuscript with Tychicus on a mission to encourage those churches. The contents of the letter don't confront any crises. Paul used this occasion to provide Christians with a basic overview of the Christian life.

OBSERVATION

Read Ephesians 1:1–14 from the NCV or the NKJV.

NCV

¹From Paul, an apostle of Christ Jesus. I am an apostle because that is what God wanted.

To God's holy people living in Ephesus, believers in Christ Jesus:

²Grace and peace to you from God our Father and the Lord Jesus Christ.

³Praise be to the God and Father of our Lord Jesus Christ. In Christ, God has given us every spiritual blessing in the heavenly world. ⁴That is, in Christ, he chose us before the world was made so that we would be his holy people—people without blame before him. ⁵Because of his love, God had already decided to make us his own children through Jesus Christ. That was what he wanted and what pleased him, ⁶and it brings praise to God because of his wonderful grace. God gave that grace to us freely, in Christ, the One he loves. ⁷In Christ we are set free by the blood of his death, and so we have forgiveness of sins. How rich is God's grace, ⁸which he has given to us so fully and freely. God, with full wisdom and understanding, ⁹let us know his secret purpose. This was what God wanted, and he planned to do it through Christ. ¹⁰His goal was to carry out his plan, when the right time came, that all things in heaven and on earth would be joined together in Christ as the head.

¹¹In Christ we were chosen to be God's people, because from the very beginning God had decided this in keeping with his plan. And he is the One who makes everything agree with what he decides and wants. ¹²We are the first people who hoped in Christ, and we were chosen so that we would bring praise to God's glory. ¹³So it is with you. When you heard the true teaching—the Good News about your salvation—you believed in Christ. And in Christ, God put his special mark of ownership on you by giving you the Holy Spirit that he had promised. ¹⁴That Holy Spirit is the guarantee that we will receive what God promised for his people until God gives full freedom to those who are his—to bring praise to God's glory.

NKJV

Paul, an apostle of Jesus Christ by the will of God,

To the saints who are in Ephesus, and faithful in Christ Jesus:

²Grace to you and peace from God our Father and the Lord Jesus Christ.

³Blessed be the God and Father of our Lord Jesus Christ, who has blessed us with every spiritual blessing in the heavenly places in Christ, ⁴just as He chose us in Him before the foundation of the world, that we should be holy and without blame before Him in love, ⁵having predestined us to adoption as sons by Jesus Christ to Himself, according to the good pleasure of His will, ⁶to the praise of the glory of His grace, by which He has made us accepted in the Beloved.

7In Him we have redemption through His blood, the forgiveness of sins, according to the riches of His grace 8which He made to abound toward us in all wisdom and prudence, 9having made known to us the mystery of His will, according to His good pleasure which He purposed in Himself, 10that in the dispensation of the fullness of the times He might gather together in one all things in Christ, both which are in heaven and which are on earth—in Him. 11In Him also we have obtained an inheritance, being predestined according to the purpose of Him who works all things according to the counsel of His will, 12that we who first trusted in Christ should be to the praise of His glory.

13In Him you also trusted, after you heard the word of truth, the gospel of your salvation; in whom also, having believed, you were sealed with the Holy Spirit of promise, 14who is the guarantee of our inheritance until the redemption of the purchased possession, to the praise of His glory.

EXPLORATION

1. What are some spiritual blessings that we have through Christ?

2. God forgives our sins through the blood of Christ. What difference does that make in our daily lives?

3. What is special about the fact that God deliberately *chooses* us as his people?

4. How does God choose his people? Do your best to anchor your answer to God's Word.

5. In what way is the Holy Spirit God's mark of ownership on us?

INSPIRATION

And you thought God adopted you because you were good looking. You thought he needed your money or your wisdom. Sorry. God adopted you simply because he wanted to. You were in his good will and pleasure. Knowing full well the trouble you would be and the price he would pay, he signed his name next to yours and changed your name to his and took you home. Your *Abba* adopted you and became your Father.

May I pause here for just a minute? Most of you are with me . . . but a couple of you are shaking your heads. I see those squinty eyes. You don't believe me, do you? You're waiting for the fine print. There's got to be a gimmick. You know life has no free lunch, so you're waiting for the check.

Your discomfort is obvious. Even here in God's living room, you never unwind. Others put on slippers, you put on a front. Others relax, you stiffen. Always on your best behavior, ever anxious that you'll slip up and God will notice and out you'll go.

I understand your anxiety. Our experience with people has taught us that what is promised and what is presented aren't always the same. And for some, the thought of trusting a heavenly Father is doubly difficult because your earthly father disappointed or mistreated you.

If such is the case, I urge you: Don't confuse your heavenly Father with the fathers you've seen on earth. Your Father in heaven isn't prone to headaches and temper tantrums. He doesn't hold you one day and hit you the next. The man who fathered you may play such games, but the God who loves you never will. (From *The Great House of God* by Max Lucado)

REACTION

6. Describe being unwanted. In what situations in life have you vividly felt that you didn't belong?

7. Describe being valued. How did you discover that you were highly regarded by someone? What did that feel like, and in what ways did it affect your actions?

8. Why does God value us? (Note Max's insight on this in the reading.)

9. What conclusions can you draw from the statement that God chose us before the foundation of the world?

10. In what ways do we bring praise to God's glory?

11. Describe someone who has exemplified God's grace to you.

LIFE LESSONS

We experience "belonging" in many temporary, shallow ways in modern life: playing on a sports team, a corporate community at work, joining exercise clubs, country clubs, book clubs, and service clubs. The attraction of these connections illustrates how badly we long to belong. What these earth-based groups offer in part, God our Father offers in whole. We long to belong because we were designed to belong. Until we know to *whom* we belong, life will always lack a sense of ultimate purpose and direction. In Christ we can experience true belonging. Acknowledging that God has chosen us and "owns" us begins a great adventure of freedom and service for Christ.

DEVOTION

Thank you, God, for choosing us. May we be spurred on by your love to do great works, yet never substitute those works for your great grace. May we always hear your voice. Keep us amazed and mesmerized by what you have done for us.

For more Bible passages on being God's child, see John 1:11–13; Romans 8:15–17; Galatians 3:26–4:7; Hebrews 12:8–11.

To complete the book of Ephesians during this twelve-part study, read Ephesians 1:1–14.

JOURNALING

What situations will I face more effectively this week if I remember that I am chosen and valued by God?

LESSON TWO

THE POWER
OF OUR
FAITH

MAX
LUCADO

REFLECTION

Power and faith rarely come together in the same sentence. People tend to think of faith as a trait that creates endurance, comfort, and perhaps influence with God. But powerful faith? Those who spend time with authentic faithful people discover there's power in faith. Or more accurately, power released by faith. Can you name two or three people you think have a powerful faith in God? What are the evidences of their faith?

SITUATION

As was his practice in most of his letters to churches, Paul prayed before, during, and after he wrote. He described in detail the way he prayed for other Christians, providing us with wonderful examples of encouraging prayer. These were not casual or canned prayers, but deep longings expressed to God on behalf of others. In this prayer Paul detailed the extraordinary power we have as believers.

OBSERVATION

Read Ephesians 1:15–23 from the NCV or the NKJV.

NCV

15That is why since I heard about your faith in the Lord Jesus and your love for all God's people, 16I have not stopped giving thanks to God for you. I always remember you in my prayers, 17asking the God of our Lord Jesus Christ, the glorious Father, to give you a spirit of wisdom and revelation so that you will know him better. 18I pray also that you will have greater understanding in your heart so you will know the hope to which he has called us and that you will know how rich and glorious are the blessings God has promised his holy people. 19And you will know that God's power is very great for us who believe. That power is the same as the great strength 20God used to raise Christ from the dead and put him at his right side in the heavenly world. 21God has put Christ over all rulers, authorities, powers, and kings, not only in this world but also in the next. 22God put everything under his power and made him the head over everything for the church, 23which is Christ's body. The church is filled with Christ, and Christ fills everything in every way.

NKJV

15Therefore I also, after I heard of your faith in the Lord Jesus and your love for all the saints, 16do not cease to give thanks for you, making mention of you in my prayers:17that the God of our Lord Jesus Christ, the Father of glory, may give to you the spirit of wisdom and revelation in the knowledge of Him, 18the eyes of your understanding being enlightened; that you may know what is the hope of His calling, what are the riches of the glory of His inheritance in the saints, 19and what is the exceeding greatness of His power toward us who believe, according to the working of His mighty power 20which He worked in Christ when He raised Him from the dead and seated Him at His right hand in the heavenly places, 21far above all principality and power and might and dominion, and every name that is named, not only in this age but also in that which is to come.

22And He put all things under His feet, and gave Him to be head over all things to the church, 23which is His body, the fullness of Him who fills all in all.

EXPLORATION

1. Why does having faith make a difference in our lives?

2. Paul prayed for the Ephesians to have a spirit of wisdom and revelation to know God better. Describe the process of knowing God better.

3. What rich and glorious blessings promised by God do you hold on to in your life?

4. The same power that raised Christ from the dead works through our faith. In what way should we be using the power of our faith?

5. If God is over all rulers, kings, and powers in this world, why do evil dictators exist?

INSPIRATION

When you believe in Christ, Christ works a miracle in you. "When you believed in Christ, he identified you as his own by giving you the Holy Spirit" (Eph. 1:13 NLT). You are permanently purified and empowered by God himself. The message of Jesus to the religious person is simple: It's not what you do. It's what I do. I have moved in. And in time you can say with Paul, "I myself no longer live, but Christ lives in me" (Gal. 2:20 NLT). You are no longer a clunker, not even a clean clunker. You are a sleek Indianapolis Motor Speedway racing machine.

If that's true, Max, why do I still sputter? If I'm born again, why do I fall so often?

Why did you fall so often after your first birth? Did you exit the womb wearing cross-trainers? Did you do the two-step on the day of your delivery? Of course not! And when you started to walk, you fell more than you stood. Should we expect anything different form our spiritual walk?

But I fall so often, I question my salvation. Again, we return to your first birth. Didn't you stumble as you were learning to walk? And when you stumbled, did you question the validity of your physical birth? Did you, as a one-year-old fresh flopped on the floor, shake your head and think, *I have fallen again. I must not be human!*

Of course not. The stumbles of a toddler do not invalidate the act of birth. And the stumbles of a Christian do not annul his spiritual birth.

Do you understand what God has done? He has deposited a Christ seed in you. As it grows, you will change. It's not that sin has no more presence in your life, but rather that sin has no more power over your life. Temptation will pester you, but temptation will not master you. What hope this brings!

Nicodemuses of the world, hear this. It's not up to you! Within you abides a budding power. Trust him.

Think of it this way. Suppose you, for most of your life, have had a heart condition. Your frail pumper restricts your activities. Each morning at work when the healthy employees take the stairs, you wait for the elevator.

But then comes the transplant. A healthy heart is placed within you. After recovery, you return to work and encounter the flight of stairs—the same flight of stairs you earlier avoided. By habit, you start for the elevator. But then you remember. You aren't the same person. You have a new heart. Within you dwells a new power.

Do you live like the old person or the new? Do you count yourself as having a new heart or old? You have a choice to make.

You might say, "I can't climb stairs; I'm too weak." Does your choice negate the presence of a new heart? Dismiss the work of the surgeon? No. Choosing the elevator would suggest only one fact—you haven't learned to trust your new power.

It takes time. But at some point you've got to try those stairs. You've got to test the new ticker. You've got to experiment with the new you. For if you don't, you will run out of steam. (From *Next Door Savior* by Max Lucado)

REACTION

6. How do God's sovereignty and man's will coexist? (As much as possible, base your answer on this lesson's passage from Ephesians.)

7. What is the relationship of our will to our salvation?

8. What about your salvation causes you to actively trust God? In what areas of life?

9. Describe God's relationship to his church, as Paul states it in this passage. (See also Ephesians 5:22–32 and Colossians 1:18–20.)

10. How would Paul describe the quality of faith you see around you today? In relation to Max's comments above, is it elevator faith or stairway faith?

11. Paul says the church is the body of Christ. In what way is the church filled with Christ?

LIFE LESSONS

Paul's prayer for the Ephesians offers a powerful outline for praying for other believers. We can ask God to grant them spiritual growth, not because they try harder but because God pours himself into them. We can pray that others will know God better. The "knowing" Paul speaks of here is not figuring God out or complete understanding, but a settling into intimacy with God. We can pray that the Holy Spirit will seal them, marking them as God's own people (1:13–14), and lead them to a fuller appreciation of the salvation they have in Jesus Christ.

DEVOTION

Blessed Lord and God, we come to you, aware that you rule our world. You became flesh, dwelled among us, saw us in our fallen state, and reached in and pulled us out. You offered us salvation; you offered us mercy. And we are ever thankful.

For more Bible passages on God's powerful salvation, see Romans 8:28–30; 1 Timothy 2:3–6; Titus 3:4–7.

To complete the book of Ephesians during this twelve-part study, read Ephesians 1:15–23.

JOURNALING

In what ways am I thankful for my salvation?

LESSON THREE

HAVE MERCY!

MAX
LUCADO

REFLECTION

Imagine you are teaching a lesson on mercy to a children's class. What illustration from your life would you use to describe what it feels like to receive mercy? How would you explain what it's like to be merciful to someone? What does mercy mean to you?

SITUATION

Having laid the foundation of our life in Christ and living through his resurrection power, Paul expounded on the theme of salvation, reviewing the merciful means that God uses to bring us into his family. He distilled the central relationship between faith, grace, and the actions/works that flow out of our salvation.

OBSERVATION

Read Ephesians 2:1–10 from the NCV or the NKJV.

NCV

¹In the past you were spiritually dead because of your sins and the things you did against God. ²Yes, in the past you lived the way the world lives, following the ruler of the evil powers that are above the earth. That same spirit is now working in those who refuse to obey God. ³In the past all of us lived like them, trying to please our sinful selves and doing all the things our bodies and minds wanted. We should have suffered God's anger because of the way we were. We were the same as all other people.

⁴But God's mercy is great, and he loved us very much. ⁵Though we were spiritually dead because of the things we did against God, he gave us new life with Christ. You have been saved by God's grace. ⁶And he raised us up with Christ and gave us a seat with him in the heavens. He did this for those in Christ Jesus ⁷so that for all future time he could show the very great riches of his grace by being kind to us in Christ Jesus. ⁸I mean that you have been saved by grace through believing. You did not save yourselves; it was a gift from God. ⁹It was not the result of your own efforts, so you cannot brag about it. ¹⁰God has made us what we are. In Christ Jesus, God made us to do good works, which God planned in advance for us to live our lives doing.

NKJV

¹And you He made alive, who were dead in trespasses and sins, ²in which you once walked according to the course of this world, according to the prince of the power of the air, the spirit who now works in the sons of disobedience, ³among whom also we all once conducted ourselves in the lusts of our flesh, fulfilling the desires of the flesh and of the mind, and were by nature children of wrath, just as the others.

⁴But God, who is rich in mercy, because of His great love with which He loved us, ⁵even when we were dead in trespasses, made us alive together with Christ (by grace you have been saved), ⁶and raised us up together, and made us sit together in the heavenly places in Christ Jesus, ⁷that in the ages to come He might show the exceeding riches of His grace in His kindness toward us in Christ Jesus. ⁸For by grace you have been saved through faith, and that not of yourselves; it is the gift of God, ⁹not of works, lest anyone should boast. ¹⁰For we are His workmanship, created in Christ Jesus for good works, which God prepared beforehand that we should walk in them.

EXPLORATION

1. What is something you did in the past but would never do now, specifically because you are a Christian? In other words, what specific changes have occurred because of Christ's presence in your life?

2. Why does sin anger God?

3. In what sense is "spiritually dead" an accurate description of life without faith in Christ?

4. Explain the relationship of Jesus to the gift of salvation.

5. Why do we sometimes perceive our salvation to be related to our own efforts?

INSPIRATION

If the Lord is the shepherd who leads the flock, goodness and mercy are the two sheepdogs that guard the rear of the flock. Goodness *and* mercy. Not goodness alone, for we are sinners in need of mercy. Not mercy alone, for we are fragile, in need of goodness. We need them both . . .

Goodness and mercy—the celestial escort of God's flock. If that duo doesn't reinforce your faith, try this phrase: "all the days of my life."

What a huge statement. Look at the size of it! Goodness and mercy follow the child of God each and every day! Think of the days that lie ahead. What do you see? Days at home with only toddlers? God will be at your side. Days in a dead-end job? He will walk you through. Days of loneliness? He will take your hand. Surely goodness and mercy shall follow me—not some, not most, not nearly all—but all the days of my life.

And what will he do during those days? (Here's my favorite word.) He will "follow" you.

What a surprising way to describe God! We're accustomed to a God who remains in one place. A God who sits enthroned in the heavens and rules and ordains. David, however, envisions a mobile and active God. Dare we do the same? Dare we envision a God who follows us? Who pursues us? Who chases us? Who tracks us down and wins us over? Who follows us with "goodness and mercy" all the days of our lives?

Isn't this the kind of God described in the Bible? (From *Traveling Light* by Max Lucado)

REACTION

6. If God were not merciful, what would our lives be like?

7. Think of a time when you had the opportunity to show mercy but didn't. Why didn't you?

8. Describe an act of mercy you have seen recently.

9. What is the danger of a faith based on works? How do you tell the difference between works-based faith and faith-based works?

10. What was your life like before you were saved?

11. How can we as Christians show the great riches of God's grace?

LIFE LESSONS

In an imperfect world we like to think that our rewards are connected to our performance. Those who don't try or don't work hard shouldn't get the same benefits as those who do try and work hard, right? But when we apply this thinking to a perfect God with absolute standards, our meager efforts don't make the grade. No matter how high our grade on a performance curve, we haven't come anywhere near perfection. Without God's mercy and grace, we're stuck in imperfect. We're stuck without hope. We're just plain stuck. God's mercy comes and gets us unstuck. His mercy saves us through Jesus Christ. And since we continue to live in an imperfect world where we continue to experience falling short, God's mercy continues to get us unstuck.

DEVOTION

Here we are, Father. We call ourselves your people, yet we carry the baggage of a week of concerns. We come to you just as we are, without trying to hide our mistakes and our weaknesses. We need your mercy and grace. Father, mend us and make us better than we could be alone.

For more Bible passages on God's mercy, see Nehemiah 9:29–31; Micah 7:18–20; Luke 6:34–36; 1 Timothy 1:15–16.

To complete the book of Ephesians during this twelve-part study, read Ephesians 2:1–10.

JOURNALING

Where can I show more mercy through my life?

L E S S O N   F O U R

FAMILY TIES AND RACIAL BLURS

MAX LUCADO

REFLECTION

In Paul's day the early Christians wrestled with prejudice and racism and pride. In our day people in the church are not perfect either. For a few moments, consider the relationships you have within the family of God. Do you put up walls and barriers? How have the good parts of these relationships and experiences shaped you as a person?

SITUATION

In most of the cities where Christianity was planted, the society could be divided into two groups: displaced Jews and everyone else (Gentiles). Ephesus was no exception. Often in these cities there was an uneasy truce between the groups for the sake of business or peace. The gospel created new unexpected tension. This was because Christianity removed the natural social and religious barriers between these groups. This was not always a welcomed development. Some wanted the "separation" maintained. Paul consistently taught that, in Christ, people from very different backgrounds could be one.

OBSERVATION

Read Ephesians 2:11–22 from the NCV or the NKJV.

NCV

11You were not born Jewish. You are the people the Jews call "uncircumcised." Those who call you "uncircumcised" call themselves "circumcised." (Their circumcision is only something they themselves do on their bodies.) 12Remember that in the past you were without Christ. You were not citizens of Israel, and you had no part in the agreements with the promise that God made to his people. You had no hope, and you did not know God. 13But now in Christ Jesus, you who were far away from God are brought near through the blood of Christ's death. 14Christ himself is our peace. He made both Jewish people and those who are not Jews one people. They were separated as if there were a wall between them, but Christ broke down that wall of hate by giving his own body. 15The Jewish law had many commands and rules, but Christ ended that law. His purpose was to make the two groups of people become one new people in him and in this way make peace. 16It was also Christ's purpose to end the hatred between the two groups, to make them into one body, and to bring them back to God. Christ did all this with his death on the cross. 17Christ came and preached peace to you who were far away from God, and to those who were near to God. 18Yes, it is through Christ we all have the right to come to the Father in one Spirit.

19Now you who are not Jewish are not foreigners or strangers any longer, but are citizens together with God's holy people. You belong to God's family. 20You are like a building that was built on the foundation of the apostles and prophets. Christ Jesus himself is the most important stone in that building, 21and that whole building is joined together in Christ. He makes it grow and become a holy temple in the Lord. 22And in Christ you, too, are being built together with the Jews into a place where God lives through the Spirit.

NKJV

11Therefore remember that you, once Gentiles in the flesh—who are called Uncircumcision by what is called the Circumcision made in the flesh by hands—12that at that time you were without Christ, being aliens from the commonwealth of Israel and strangers from the covenants of promise, having no hope and without God in the world. 13But now in Christ Jesus you who once were far off have been brought near by the blood of Christ.

14For He Himself is our peace, who has made both one, and has broken down the middle wall of separation, 15having abolished in His flesh the enmity, that is, the law of commandments contained in ordinances, so as to create in Himself one new man from the two, thus making peace, 16and that He might reconcile them both to God in one body through the cross, thereby putting to death the enmity. 17And He came and preached peace to you who were afar off and to those who were near. 18For through Him we both have access by one Spirit to the Father.

19Now, therefore, you are no longer strangers and foreigners, but fellow citizens with the saints and members of the household of God, 20having been built on the foundation of the apostles and prophets, Jesus Christ Himself being the chief cornerstone, 21in whom the whole building, being joined together, grows into a holy temple in the Lord, 22in whom you also are being built together for a dwelling place of God in the Spirit.

EXPLORATION

1. List some characteristics that would have separated Jews and Gentiles.

2. What is Paul describing when he says that Christ is our "peace"?

3. Before Christ's death the Jewish nation judged their righteousness by their obedience to numerous laws, regulations, and sacrifices. In what way did Christ's life and death challenge that concept of righteousness?

4. Christ's death and resurrection changed the way we approach God—from his creatures to his children. Describe the difference. (For additional help, look at Romans 8:13–17.)

5. This passage describes the church of Christ as a building of many stones. How does that analogy work well in describing the church today?

INSPIRATION

We specialize in "I am right" rallies. We write books about what the other does wrong. We major in finding gossip and become experts in unveiling weaknesses. We split into little huddles and then, God forbid, we split again . . .

Are our differences that divisive? Are our opinions that obtrusive? Are our walls that wide? Is it *that* impossible to find a common cause?

"May they all be one," Jesus prayed.

One. Not one in groups of two thousand. But one in One. *One* church. *One* faith. *One* Lord. Not Baptist, not Methodist, not Adventist. Just Christian. No denominations. No hierarchies. No traditions. Just Christ.

Too idealistic? Impossible to achieve? I don't think so. Harder things have been done, you know. For example, once upon a tree, a Creator gave his life for his creation. Maybe all we need are a few hearts that are willing to follow suit. (From *No Wonder They Call Him the Savior* by Max Lucado)

REACTION

6. What were the racial implications of the peace Christ brought?

7. One of the efforts of Christ was to end racially based and culturally based hatred. In what ways can the church today help that effort?

8. List the best benefits you have discovered in belonging to God's family.

9. How did Christ's death give us the right to come to God as our father?

10. What barriers to unity in Christ have you seen in your own church?

11. What's important about the fact that Jesus is the cornerstone of the church? How can that fact lead to more unity among believers?

LIFE LESSONS

Jesus ended his Sermon on the Mount with the claim that trusting and obeying him was like building a house on a rock (see Matthew 7:24–27). Paul echoes that point in his teaching about the church. Everything rests on Jesus Christ. Faithfulness to him determines all actions and decisions. Jesus is the ultimate equalizer. In a world where we are proud of what makes us different (better) from others, Jesus offers a place where we meet as equals. He declares that the walls we build are irrelevant and wants to remove them. Jesus doesn't offer an alternative; he comes to us with the original plan and a way to get back to it. He is the way.

DEVOTION

Father, as we set about the task of being your people, we pray that you'll help us. May we glorify your name. May we be open-minded. May we be sincere. May we be willing to change and grow. We thank you, Lord, for the privilege of being in your family.

For more Bible passages on God's family, see Acts 13:44–48; Romans 8:13–17; 2 Corinthians 5:14–15; Galatians 3:26–29; 1 Timothy 2:3–4.

To complete the book of Ephesians during this twelve-part study, read Ephesians 2:11–22.

JOURNALING

What are my privileges and responsibilities in belonging to God's family?

LESSON FIVE

GOD HAD A
SECRET?

MAX
LUCADO

REFLECTION

Secrets and mysteries are selective. They are only secrets and mysteries to the ones who don't know. God has always known his plans. And he has graciously shared them with his creation in his timing. A long-kept, then revealed secret can have wonderful effects! Think of a time when someone gave you a surprise party or gift he or she had worked on in secret. How did you feel when you received it?

SITUATION

It's amazing how Paul spoke so confidently of the oneness of believers in Jesus. One of the primary reasons for his assurance was his own training in the Old Testament Scriptures. He realized that the gospel message, with its inclusion of the Gentiles, had always been there, hiding in plain sight. But it took Jesus Christ to finally reveal it to the world. Paul then described the unfolding of God's plan, once mysterious, but now an open secret.

OBSERVATION

Read Ephesians 3:1–13 from the NCV or the NKJV.

NCV

¹So I, Paul, am a prisoner of Christ Jesus for you who are not Jews. ²Surely you have heard that God gave me this work through his grace to help you. ³He let me know his secret by showing it to me. I have already written a little about this. ⁴If you read what I wrote then, you can see that I truly understand the secret about the Christ. ⁵People who lived in other times were not told that secret. But now, through the Spirit, God has shown that secret to his holy apostles and prophets. ⁶This is that secret: that through the Good News those who are not Jews will share with the Jews in God's blessing. They belong to the same body, and they share together in the promise that God made in Christ Jesus.

⁷By God's special gift of grace given to me through his power, I became a servant to tell that Good News. ⁸I am the least important of all God's people, but God gave me this gift—to tell those who are not Jews the Good News about the riches of Christ, which are too great to understand fully. ⁹And God gave me the work of telling all people about the plan for his secret, which has been hidden in him since the beginning of time. He is the One who created everything. ¹⁰His purpose was that through the church all the rulers and powers in the heavenly world will now know God's wisdom, which has so many forms. ¹¹This agrees with the purpose God had since the beginning of time, and he carried out his plan through Christ Jesus our Lord. ¹²In Christ we can come before God with freedom and without fear. We can do this through faith in Christ. ¹³So I ask you not to become discouraged because of the sufferings I am having for you. My sufferings are for your glory.

NKJV

¹For this reason I, Paul, the prisoner of Christ Jesus for you Gentiles—²if indeed you have heard of the dispensation of the grace of God which was given to me for you, ³how that by revelation He made known to me the mystery (as I have briefly written already, ⁴by which, when you read, you may understand my knowledge in the mystery of Christ), ⁵which in other ages was not made known to the sons of men, as it has now been revealed by the Spirit to His holy apostles and prophets: ⁶that the Gentiles should be fellow heirs, of the same body, and partakers of His promise in Christ through the gospel, ⁷of which I became a minister according to the gift of the grace of God given to me by the effective working of His power.

⁸To me, who am less than the least of all the saints, this grace was given, that I should preach among the Gentiles the unsearchable riches of Christ, ⁹and to make all see what is the fellowship of the mystery, which from the beginning of the ages has been hidden in God who created all things through Jesus Christ; ¹⁰to the intent that now the manifold wisdom of God might be made known by the church to the principalities and powers in the heavenly places, ¹¹according to the eternal purpose which He accomplished in Christ Jesus our Lord, ¹²in whom we have boldness and access with confidence through faith in Him. ¹³Therefore I ask that you do not lose heart at my tribulations for you, which is your glory.

EXPLORATION

1. Paul, a Jew, became a missionary to the Gentiles at a time when the Jewish people found their identity in the fact that they were God's only chosen people. What consequences might Paul have had to pay for his actions? (See, for example, 2 Corinthians 11:16–33.)

2. Why did Paul describe God's plan (to offer all people salvation) as a "secret"?

3. Why might the Jewish leaders have felt threatened by Paul's insistence that God included all people in his promise of salvation?

4. Give your ideas about why Paul said he was the least important of all God's people.

5. Through Christ, human beings can come to God in freedom and without fear. In what ways is that different from coming to God before Christ's incarnation?

INSPIRATION

What would it be like to become flesh?

This question surfaced as I was golfing recently. Waiting my turn to putt, I squatted down to clean my ball and noticed a mountain of ants beside it. Must have been dozens of them, all over each other. A pyramid of motion at least half an inch tall.

I don't know what you think when you see ants on a green as you are waiting to putt. But here is what I thought: *Why are you guys all bunched up? You have the whole green. Why, the entire golf course in yours to spread out in.* Then it occurred to me. These ants are nervous. Who could blame them? They live under a constant meteor shower. Every few minutes a dimpled orb comes crashing into their world. *Bam! Bam! Bam!* Just when the bombing stops, the mallet-swinging giants arrive. If you survive their feet and sticks, they roll a meteor at you. A golf green is no place for an ant.

So I tried to help them. Leaning down where they could hear me, I invited, "Come on, follow me. We'll find a nice spot in the rough. I know it well." Not one looked in my direction. "Hey, ants!" Still no reply. Then I realized, I don't speak their language. I don't speak Ant. Pretty fluent in the idiom of Uncle, but I don't speak Ant.

So what could I do to reach them? Only one thing. I needed to become an ant. Go from six feet two inches to teeny-weeny. From 200-plus pounds to tenths of an ounce. Swap my big world for their tiny one. Give up burgers and start eating grass. "No thanks," I said. Besides, it was my turn to putt.

Love goes the distance . . . and Christ traveled from limitless eternity to be confined by time in order to become one of us. He didn't have to. He could have given up. At any step along the way he could have called it quits . . . He didn't, because he is love. And "love . . . endures all things" (I Cor. 13:4–7 NKJV). He endured the distance. (From *A Love Worth Giving* by Max Lucado)

REACTION

6. The secret of God's salvation is really too great for us to fully understand. On what, then, is our faith in God's salvation and love based?

7. What are some examples in your everyday world of things that you use or benefit from, even though you do not understand them?

8. In what ways would you describe God's love to someone who has never heard of God?

9. What kind of suffering was Paul referring to in the last verse of this passage?

10. In what ways is God's salvation through Christ not a secret at all?

11. How have you experienced the "riches of Christ" in your life?

LIFE LESSONS

We function every day making use of items whose workings we don't understand. We drive cars, use copiers, type on computers, and perform many other tasks with only a dim sense of what makes a car run, a copier copy, or a computer compute. The same is true of the mystery of being in Christ. We don't have to fully understand God's grace before we take full advantage of it. We don't have to comprehend (and we certainly never will on this side of eternity) why God loves us, but that should never keep us from experiencing and relishing in his love.

DEVOTION

Father, we look at your plan and see that it's all based on your love, not on our performance. Help us understand that. Teach us to be captivated by your love. Allow us to be overwhelmed by your grace. Remind us to live grateful lives. Amen.

For more Bible passages on God's provision through Christ, see John 3:16; 15:12; Romans 5:8; 8:35–37; 1 John 3:1.

To complete the book of Ephesians during this twelve-part study, read Ephesians 3:1–13.

JOURNALING

In what situations or times in my life have I felt the most loved by God?

LESSON SIX

THE
AMAZING
LOVE OF
CHRIST

MAX
LUCADO

REFLECTION

You can't see it; you can't touch it; but love is a powerful force. When was the last time you were truly amazed by someone's love for you? How would you describe that experience?

SITUATION

Among the personal traits that Paul reveals in his letters, at least one stands out clearly: he was always praying. This letter began with prayer, and now, as Paul concludes the teaching part of his message, he again prays for the Ephesians, expressing his highest wishes for them in their walk with God.

OBSERVATION

Read Ephesians 3:14–21 from the NCV or the NKJV.

NCV

[14]*So I bow in prayer before the Father* [15]*from whom every family in heaven and on earth gets its true name.* [16]*I ask the Father in his great glory to give you the power to be strong inwardly through his Spirit.* [17]*I pray that Christ will live in your hearts by faith and that your life will be strong in love and be built on love.* [18]*And I pray that you and all God's holy people will have the power to understand the greatness of Christ's love—how wide and how long and how high and how deep that love is.* [19]*Christ's love is greater than anyone can ever know, but I pray that you will be able to know that love. Then you can be filled with the fullness of God.*

[20]*With God's power working in us, God can do much, much more than anything we can ask or imagine.* [21]*To him be glory in the church and in Christ Jesus for all time, forever and ever. Amen.*

NKJV

[14]*For this reason I bow my knees to the Father of our Lord Jesus Christ,* [15]*from whom the whole family in heaven and earth is named,* [16]*that He would grant you, according to the riches of His glory, to be strengthened with might through His Spirit in the inner man,* [17]*that Christ may dwell in your hearts through faith; that you, being rooted and grounded in love,* [18]*may be able to comprehend with all the saints what is the width and length and depth and height—*[19]*to know the love of Christ which passes knowledge; that you may be filled with all the fullness of God.*

[20]*Now to Him who is able to do exceedingly abundantly above all that we ask or think, according to the power that works in us,* [21]*to Him be glory in the church by Christ Jesus to all generations, forever and ever. Amen.*

EXPLORATION

1. In what way does every family on heaven and earth get their true name from God?

2. Paul prayed that the Ephesians would be "strong inwardly" through Christ's Spirit. Describe a person who fits that description.

3. What are the hallmarks of our families and churches when we each build our lives on love, as Paul prayed?

4. In what ways can we know Christ's love, even though we don't understand it?

5. How can we be sure God's power, rather than our own strength, is working through us?

INSPIRATION

Does God love you? Behold the cross, and behold your answer.

God the Son died for you. Who could have imagined such a gift? At the time Martin Luther was having his Bible printed in Germany, a printer's daughter encountered God's love. No one had told her about Jesus. Toward God she felt no emotion but fear. One day she gathered pieces of fallen Scripture from the floor. On one paper she found the words "For God so loved the world, that he gave . . . " The rest of the verse had not yet been printed. Still, what she saw was enough to move her. The thought that God would give anything moved her from fear to joy. Her mother noticed the change of attitude. When asked the cause of her happiness, the daughter produced the crumpled piece of partial verse from her pocket. The mother read it and asked, "What did he give?" The child was perplexed for a moment and then answered, "I do not know. But if he loves us well enough to give us anything, we should not be afraid of him."

"[God the Son] loved us and gave himself up for us as a fragrant offering and sacrifice to God" (Eph. 5:2 NIV). What species of devotion is this? The holiness of God demanded a sinless sacrifice, and the only sinless sacrifice was God the Son. And since God's love never fails to pay the price, he did. God loves you with an unfailing love. (From *It's Not About Me* by Max Lucado)

REACTION

6. Describe a time when you felt "touched" or surrounded by the love of Christ.

7. List some ways Christ showed his love and compassion during his earthly ministry. (For examples of Jesus' compassion, you can look at his responses to the crowds in Matthew 9:36–38; 14:13–14; and 15:29–39. Also look at his interactions with the two blind men in Matthew 20:29–34, with the leper in Mark 1:40–42, with the grieving mother in Luke 7:11–15, and with Jairus and the hemorrhaging woman in Luke 8:40–56.)

8. List some ministries in the church today that reflect the way Jesus cared for the people around him.

9. How can we live our lives so that we are most likely to experience the love of Christ? (Keep in mind that this question concerns our perception of God's love, not whether he loves us or not. While the choices we make will affect that perception, there is nothing a believer can do to remove him or her from it.)

10. To what do you compare the magnitude of Christ's love?

11. How can you build your life on that love and share it with others?

LIFE LESSONS

We can't force people to believe that God loves them, and they can't stop *us* from loving them. The underlying power of Paul's words to the Ephesians came from the convincing power of the Holy Spirit and from the compassionate power of Paul's commitment to them. Paul never stopped being amazed that God would use him; he never stopped inviting others to be amazed that God would love them. God's love has a width, length, height, and depth, but we will never reach the end of it. Our capacity to experience God's love will be exhausted and full long before God's capacity to give it is strained. The picture of having Christ "dwell" inside us by faith presents us with compelling and comforting possibilities. What Christ does in us and through us will always be "exceedingly abundantly above all that we ask or think" (Eph. 3:20 NKJV).

DEVOTION

We're not perfect, Father, but we are yours. We claim your salvation and your grace. We ask you to make us every day into the image of Jesus Christ. Help us to walk this earth in love as he did. We are amazed at such mercy that forgives us time and time again. Thank you.

For more Bible passages on Christ's love, see Matthew 8:14–16; 9:35–37; 14:13–14; 20:29–34; 23:37; Mark 10:13–16; Luke 7:12–13; 22:49–51; John 11:33–35.

To complete the book of Ephesians during this twelve-part study, read Ephesians 3:14–21.

JOURNALING

How can I be more like Christ in the way I show love to the people around me?

BODY PARTS EVERYWHERE

MAX LUCADO

REFLECTION

Injuries, broken bones, and loss of limb can have a devastating effect on a person's body. Even a simple blister on a toe or a paper cut on a finger quickly reminds us how much we use every part of our anatomy to function. Consider for a few moments how valuable each part of your body is to you. Why is the body of Christ such a meaningful analogy for the church?

SITUATION

Paul used written messages to continue his work as an apostle while he was in prison. Apparently his incarceration in Rome still allowed him visitors, and he made maximum use of them as messengers to carry on his ministry throughout the Roman Empire. As he does in many of his letters, Paul devoted the first part to doctrinal teaching and the second part to practical application. He's saying, "If you will agree with what I've just told you, the following choices and actions will be required."

OBSERVATION

Read Ephesians 4:1–16 from the NCV or the NKJV.

NCV

¹*I am in prison because I belong to the Lord. God chose you to be his people, so I urge you now to live the life to which God called you.* ²*Always be humble, gentle, and patient, accepting each other in love.* ³*You are joined together with peace through the Spirit, so make every effort to continue together in this way.* ⁴*There is one body and one Spirit, and God called you to have one hope.* ⁵*There is one Lord, one faith, and one baptism.* ⁶*There is one God and Father of everything. He rules everything and is everywhere and is in everything.*

⁷*Christ gave each one of us the special gift of grace, showing how generous he is.* ⁸*That is why it says in the Scriptures,*

> *"When he went up to the heights,*
>
> *he led a parade of captives,*
>
> *and he gave gifts to people."*

⁹*When it says, "He went up," what does it mean? It means that he first came down to the earth.* ¹⁰*So Jesus came down, and he is the same One who went up above all the heaven. Christ did that to fill everything with his presence.* ¹¹*And Christ gave gifts to people—he made some to be apostles, some to be prophets, some to go and tell the Good News, and some to have the work of caring for and teaching God's people.* ¹²*Christ gave those gifts to prepare God's holy people for the work of serving, to make the body of Christ stronger.* ¹³*This work must continue until we are all joined together in the same faith and in the same knowledge of the Son of God. We must become like a mature person, growing until we become like Christ and have his perfection.*

¹⁴*Then we will no longer be babies. We will not be tossed about like a ship that the waves carry one way and then another. We will not be influenced by every new teaching we hear from people who are trying to fool us. They make plans and try any kind of trick to fool people into following the wrong path.* ¹⁵*No! Speaking the truth with love, we will grow up in every way into Christ, who is the head.* ¹⁶*The whole body depends on Christ, and all the parts of the body are joined and held together. Each part does its own work to make the whole body grow and be strong with love.*

NKJV

¹*I, therefore, the prisoner of the Lord, beseech you to walk worthy of the calling with which you were called,* ²*with all lowliness and gentleness, with longsuffering, bearing with one another in love,* ³*endeavoring to keep the unity of the Spirit in the bond of peace.* ⁴*There is one body and one Spirit, just as you were called in one hope of your calling;* ⁵*one Lord, one faith, one baptism;* ⁶*one God and Father of all, who is above all, and through all, and in you all.*

7*But to each one of us grace was given according to the measure of Christ's gift.* 8*Therefore He says:*

> *"When He ascended on high,*
>
> *He led captivity captive,*
>
> *And gave gifts to men."*

9*(Now this, "He ascended"—what does it mean but that He also first descended into the lower parts of the earth?* 10*He who descended is also the One who ascended far above all the heavens, that He might fill all things.)*

11*And He Himself gave some to be apostles, some prophets, some evangelists, and some pastors and teachers,* 12*for the equipping of the saints for the work of ministry, for the edifying of the body of Christ,* 13*till we all come to the unity of the faith and of the knowledge of the Son of God, to a perfect man, to the measure of the stature of the fullness of Christ;* 14*that we should no longer be children, tossed to and fro and carried about with every wind of doctrine, by the trickery of men, in the cunning craftiness of deceitful plotting,* 15*but, speaking the truth in love, may grow up in all things into Him who is the head—Christ—*16*from whom the whole body, joined and knit together by what every joint supplies, according to the effective working by which every part does its share, causes growth of the body for the edifying of itself in love.*

EXPLORATION

1. In what ways would you describe the life God calls us to live?

2. List some ways we can accept one another and bear with one another in love. How is this acceptance affected when we encounter someone we don't like?

3. This passage tells us that we each have a special gift of grace. Have you identified your own gift of grace? If not, what steps can you take to do so?

4. The purpose of our gifts is to grow to maturity in Christ. In what ways do the gifts you have identified help you do that?

5. This passage compares the church to a body and Christ to the head of the body. What part of the body are you?

INSPIRATION

An amazing dynamic occurs when we come to worship with a heart of worship . . . Your heartfelt worship is a missionary appeal. Let unbelievers hear the passion of your voice or see the sincerity in your face, and they will be changed. Peter was. When Peter saw the worship of Jesus, he said, "Lord, it is good that we are here. If you want, I will put up three tents here—one for you, one for Moses, and one for Elijah" (Matt. 17:4 NCV) . . . He didn't understand that God wants hearts and not tents, but at least he was moved to give something. Why? Because he saw the transfigured face of Christ.

The same happens in churches today. When people see us giving heartfelt praise to God—when they hear our worship—they are intrigued. They want to see who's in charge! Sparks from our fire tend to ignite dry hearts.

I experienced something similar in Brazil. Our house was only blocks away from the largest soccer stadium in the world. At least once a week Maracana stadium would be packed with screaming soccer fans. Initially I was not numbered among them, but their enthusiasm was contagious. I wanted to see what they were so excited about. By the time I left Rio, I was a soccer convert and could shout with the best of them.

Seekers may not understand all that happens in a house of worship. They may not understand the meaning of a song or the significance of the communion, but they know joy when they see it. And when they see your face changed, they may want to see God's face. (From *Just Like Jesus Devotional* by Max Lucado)

REACTION

6. How do church staff members equip us to do God's work? Who contributes to worship?

7. Describe the Spirit-filled life. (See also Galatians 5:16–26.)

8. In what ways should we be using our gifts to reach others for Christ?

9. What does it mean to be a spiritual baby?

10. How does Christ function with the church as does the head on a body?

11. What keeps us from humility, gentleness, and patience? (A passage like Colossians 3:1–17 may offer some help.)

LIFE LESSONS

The Christian life means following the One who calls us. That life has a basic outline, sketched by God. It can be described as a central collection of beliefs and gifts. The beliefs are shared in common; the gifts are given individually for the common good. The daily challenge of the Christian life is to participate in life in a worthy way because of all that we have been given in Christ. All believers contribute to the body of Christ. Some of their specific roles, primarily those in leadership, require faithfulness, courage, and the cooperation of those being led. The life challenge for a Christian involves a mixture of personal spiritual responsibility and willing cooperation with other believers. We share our gift(s) and benefit from theirs.

DEVOTION

Father, how holy and great is your promise. You've been so good to us and have gifted us richly. Renew our vision; help us to see heaven. Help us to be busy about the right business: the business of serving you.

For more Bible passages on the purpose of our gifts, see Romans 12:3–6; 1 Corinthians 12:12; 14:26; 1 Timothy 4:14; 2 Timothy 1:6.

To complete the book of Ephesians during this twelve-part study, read Ephesians 4:1–16.

JOURNALING

How can I use my gifts this week for God's glory?

LESSON EIGHT

THE POWER
OF WORDS

MAX
LUCADO

REFLECTION

Think of a time when someone's careless words hurt you (or vice versa). What was the immediate effect on both of you? How was the offense resolved?

SITUATION

After revealing the parts and purpose of the body of Christ, Paul wrote about the influence of the outside world on those in the body of Christ. The habits, attitudes, and sins of the world must be "put off" by those who are seeking to live out their calling within Christ's body.

OBSERVATION

Read Ephesians 4:17–32 from the NCV or the NKJV.

NCV

17In the Lord's name, I tell you this. Do not continue living like those who do not believe. Their thoughts are worth nothing. 18They do not understand, and they know nothing, because they refuse to listen. So they cannot have the life that God gives. 19They have lost all feeling of shame, and they use their lives for doing evil. They continually want to do all kinds of evil. 20But what you learned in Christ was not like this. 21I know that you heard about him, and you are in him, so you were taught the truth that is in Jesus. 22You were taught to leave your old self—to stop living the evil way you lived before. That old self becomes worse, because people are fooled by the evil things they want to do. 23But you were taught to be made new in your hearts, 24to become a new person. That new person is made to be like God—made to be truly good and holy.

25So you must stop telling lies. Tell each other the truth, because we all belong to each other in the same body. 26When you are angry, do not sin, and be sure to stop being angry before the end of the day. 27Do not give the devil a way to defeat you. 28Those who are stealing must stop stealing and start working. They should earn an honest living for themselves. Then they will have something to share with those who are poor.

29When you talk, do not say harmful things, but say what people need—words that will help others become stronger. Then what you say will do good to those who listen to you. 30And do not make the Holy Spirit sad. The Spirit is God's proof that you belong to him. God gave you the Spirit to show that God will make you free when the final day comes. 31Do not be bitter or angry or mad. Never shout angrily or say things to hurt others. Never do anything evil. 32Be kind and loving to each other, and forgive each other just as God forgave you in Christ.

NKJV

17This I say, therefore, and testify in the Lord, that you should no longer walk as the rest of the Gentiles walk, in the futility of their mind, 18having their understanding darkened, being alienated from the life of God, because of the ignorance that is in them, because of the blindness of their heart; 19who, being past feeling, have given themselves over to lewdness, to work all uncleanness with greediness.

20But you have not so learned Christ, 21if indeed you have heard Him and have been taught by Him, as the truth is in Jesus:22that you put off, concerning your former conduct, the old man which grows corrupt according to the deceitful lusts, 23and be renewed in the spirit of your mind, 24and that you put on the new man which was created according to God, in true righteousness and holiness.

25Therefore, putting away lying, "Let each one of you speak truth with his neighbor," for we are members of one another. 26"Be angry, and do not sin": do not let the sun go down on your wrath, 27nor give place to the devil. 28Let him who stole steal no longer, but rather let him labor, working with his hands what is good, that he may have something to give him who has need. 29Let no corrupt word proceed out of your mouth, but what is good for necessary edification, that it may impart grace to the hearers. 30And do not grieve the Holy Spirit of God, by whom you were sealed for the day of redemption. 31Let all bitterness, wrath, anger, clamor, and evil speaking be put away from you, with all malice. 32And be kind to one another, tenderhearted, forgiving one another, even as God in Christ forgave you.

EXPLORATION

1. Describe some evidences in our culture of a loss of shame.

2. Define the "old self." What are we to "put off" when we become followers of Jesus?

3. What is the difference between the "old self" and the "new self"?

4. In what ways do we give the devil a way to defeat us (v. 27)?

5. This passage says we are not to be unkind with our words. What are we to do with our words?

INSPIRATION

Insensitivity makes a wound that heals slowly.

If someone hurts your feelings intentionally, you know how to react. You know the source of the pain. But if someone accidentally bruises your soul, it's difficult to know how to respond.

Someone at work criticizes the new boss who also happens to be your dear friend. "Oh, I'm sorry—I forgot the two of you were so close."

A joke is told at a party about overweight people. You're overweight. You hear the joke. You smile politely while your heart sinks.

What was intended to be a reprimand for a decision or action becomes a personal attack. "You have a history of poor decisions, John."

Someone chooses to wash your dirty laundry in public. "Sue, is it true that you and Jim are separated?"

Insensitive comments. Thoughts that should have remained thoughts. Feelings which had no business being expressed. Opinions carelessly tossed like a grenade into a crowd.

And if you were to tell the one who threw these thoughtless darts about the pain they caused, his response would be "Oh, but I had no intention . . . I didn't realize you were so sensitive!" or "I forgot you were here."

In a way, the words are comforting, until you stop to think about them (which is not recommended). For when you start to think about insensitive slurs, you realize they come from an infamous family whose father has breeded generations of pain. His name? Egotism. His children? Three sisters: Disregard, disrespect, and disappointment.

These three witches have combined to poison countless relationships and break innumerable hearts. Listed among their weapons are Satan's cruelest artillery: gossip, accusations, resentment, impatience, and on and on . . .

God's Word has strong medicine for those who carelessly wag their tongues. The message is clear: He who dares to call himself God's ambassador is not afforded the luxury of idle words. Excuses such as "I didn't know you were here" or "I didn't realize this was so touchy" are shallow when they come from those who claim to be followers and imitators of the Great Physician. We have an added responsibility to guard our tongues. (From *God Came Near* by Max Lucado)

REACTION

6. Why do we say things to hurt others, even though God clearly tells us not to in this passage?

7. Why does it feel good at times to put others down?

8. How does God view our actions when we disregard or disrespect one another?

9. Is there a way to rid our lives of bitterness and anger? (Note: Ephesians 4:22–24 provides us with a formula for growth—in the area of bitterness and anger, as well as others. First, we are told to leave our "old self" (NCV) and stop doing the things that accompany it. Then we are told to be made new in our hearts; Romans 12:2 tells us that this happens as we renew our minds. As we fill our minds with the truths of God's Word, our hearts are changed. Next, we are told to become a "new person" (NCV) and start doing the things that accompany it, such as being kind and loving. Ephesians 4:31–32 gives us specifics; we are not only told what we should stop doing but also what we should start doing instead. So, how does this affect bitterness and anger?)

10. What kinds of words do others need from us?

11. How are we fooled by the evil things we want to do?

LIFE LESSONS

The need to be aware of and alter our speech patterns offers us one of the most obvious areas for spiritual growth. Paul begins with that area in laying out a "training plan" for personal transformation. Honesty with ourselves and with others becomes a foundation for other changes in life. Without personal integrity, the capacity even to acknowledge other problem areas will be severely limited. God's Word goes a long way to eliminate any guessing about areas that we need to address as we "walk worthy" of our calling (Eph. 4:1 NKJV).

DEVOTION

Father, we invite your assistance and guidance and powerful indwelling. We do not have the strength in ourselves to be transformed into your likeness and not be conformed to this world. Teach us to speak with your voice and love with your love.

For more Bible passages on speech that pleases God, see Proverbs 16:24; 25:11; Ecclesiastes 10:12; Isaiah 50:4; Ephesians 4:29; Colossians 4:6.

To complete the book of Ephesians during this twelve-part study, read Ephesians 4:17–32.

JOURNALING

How do I disregard or disrespect others through my words?

LESSON NINE

CHOOSING
TO WALK IN
THE LIGHT

MAX
LUCADO

REFLECTION

Part of walking in God's light means being wise. Authentic wisdom has its feet planted right in the middle of real life. Wisdom is pithy, practical, and shows a keen understanding of God's ways and character expressed throughout his creation. Think of the wisest people you know. List some of the evidences of wisdom in life. Consider what they share in common and how each is distinct from the others.

SITUATION

The analogy of "walking" is a good one for the Christian life. Paul encouraged the Ephesians to walk worthy of Christ, honoring him in what they did and did not do. Paul expands on that analogy, showing how God's children are to walk in love, light, and wisdom.

OBSERVATION

Read Ephesians 5:1–20 from the NCV or the NKJV.

NCV

¹You are God's children whom he loves, so try to be like him. ²Live a life of love just as Christ loved us and gave himself for us as a sweet-smelling offering and sacrifice to God.

³But there must be no sexual sin among you, or any kind of evil or greed. Those things are not right for God's holy people. ⁴Also, there must be no evil talk among you, and you must not speak foolishly or tell evil jokes. These things are not right for you. Instead, you should be giving thanks to God. ⁵You can be sure of this: No one will have a place in the kingdom of Christ and of God who sins sexually, or does evil things, or is greedy. Anyone who is greedy is serving a false god.

⁶Do not let anyone fool you by telling you things that are not true, because these things will bring God's anger on those who do not obey him. ⁷So have nothing to do with them. ⁸In the past you were full of darkness, but now you are full of light in the Lord. So live like children who belong to the light. ⁹Light brings every kind of goodness, right living, and truth. ¹⁰Try to learn what pleases the Lord. ¹¹Have nothing to do with the things done in darkness, which are not worth anything. But show that they are wrong. ¹²It is shameful even to talk about what those people do in secret. ¹³But the light makes all things easy to see, ¹⁴and everything that is made easy to see can become light. This is why it is said:

> "Wake up, sleeper!
>
> Rise from death,
>
> and Christ will shine on you."

¹⁵So be very careful how you live. Do not live like those who are not wise, but live wisely. ¹⁶Use every chance you have for doing good, because these are evil times. ¹⁷So do not be foolish but learn what the Lord wants you to do. ¹⁸Do not be drunk with wine, which will ruin you, but be filled with the Spirit. ¹⁹Speak to each other with psalms, hymns, and spiritual songs, singing and making music in your hearts to the Lord. ²⁰Always give thanks to God the Father for everything, in the name of our Lord Jesus Christ.

NKJV

¹*Therefore be imitators of God as dear children. ²And walk in love, as Christ also has loved us and given Himself for us, an offering and a sacrifice to God for a sweet-smelling aroma.*

³*But fornication and all uncleanness or covetousness, let it not even be named among you, as is fitting for saints; ⁴neither filthiness, nor foolish talking, nor coarse jesting, which are not fitting, but rather giving of thanks. ⁵For this you know, that no fornicator, unclean person, nor covetous man, who is an idolater, has any inheritance in the kingdom of Christ and God. ⁶Let no one deceive you with empty words, for because of these things the wrath of God comes upon the sons of disobedience. ⁷Therefore do not be partakers with them.*

⁸*For you were once darkness, but now you are light in the Lord. Walk as children of light ⁹(for the fruit of the Spirit is in all goodness, righteousness, and truth), ¹⁰finding out what is acceptable to the Lord. ¹¹And have no fellowship with the unfruitful works of darkness, but rather expose them. ¹²For it is shameful even to speak of those things which are done by them in secret. ¹³But all things that are exposed are made manifest by the light, for whatever makes manifest is light. ¹⁴Therefore He says:*

> *"Awake, you who sleep,*
>
> *Arise from the dead,*
>
> *And Christ will give you light."*

¹⁵*See then that you walk circumspectly, not as fools but as wise, ¹⁶redeeming the time, because the days are evil.*

¹⁷*Therefore do not be unwise, but understand what the will of the Lord is. ¹⁸And do not be drunk with wine, in which is dissipation; but be filled with the Spirit, ¹⁹speaking to one another in psalms and hymns and spiritual songs, singing and making melody in your heart to the Lord, ²⁰giving thanks always for all things to God the Father in the name of our Lord Jesus Christ,*

EXPLORATION

1. Compare and contrast a life that is full of darkness and a life that is full of light.

2. What kinds of elements would make a joke "evil" or foolish (v. 4 NCV)?

3. This passage instructs us to try to learn what pleases God. What does this have to do with walking in love?

4. Why is it shameful even to talk about the evil others do in secret?

5. We probably all know some signs of being drunk with wine. What are some signs of being filled with the Spirit?

INSPIRATION

For an hour I was in the wrong hotel. And you know what?

I *felt* as though I was in the right place. Had you asked me what I was doing eating a free meal in the wrong hotel, I would have looked at you as if you were wearing hockey clothes in the Amazon. "You're crazy."

Not once did I lift my head and furrow my brow and think, *This place feels funny.* I didn't. It *felt* fine. But my feelings were wrong. My key card proved them wrong. The room number proved them wrong. The manager, had she been asked, could have proved them wrong. No matter how much I felt as though I was in the right place, I was not. And no mountain of feelings could change that.

I wonder if you've ever made the same mistake. Not with a hotel, but with love. Have you ever made decisions about your relationships based on your feelings instead of facts? When it comes to love, feelings rule the day. Emotions guide the ship. Goose bumps call the shots. But should they? Can feelings be trusted? Can a relationship feel right but be wrong? Heads are nodding.

A single mom is nodding.

A college student with a broken heart is nodding.

The fellow who fell in love with a figure that could cause a twelve-car pileup is nodding.

Feelings can fool you. Yesterday I spoke with a teenage girl who is puzzled by the lack of feelings she has for a guy. Before they started dating, she was wild about him. The minute he showed interest in her, however, she lost interest.

I'm thinking also about a young mom. Being a parent isn't as romantic as she anticipated. Diapers and midnight feedings aren't any fun, and she's feeling guilty because they aren't. *Am I low on love?* she wonders.

How do you answer such questions? Ever wish you had a way to assess the quality of your affections? A DNA test for love? Paul offers us one: "Love does not delight in evil but rejoices with the truth" (1 Cor. 13:6 NIV). In this verse lies the test for love. (From *A Love Worth Giving* by Max Lucado)

REACTION

6. Describe the message of hope in the gospel of Jesus Christ, particularly as it has to do with love.

7. What are the signs of a life lived apart from God?

8. What keeps us from beginning again (or going on), when we have every opportunity through God's grace?

9. Explain how greed becomes idolatry.

10. How can we grow in wisdom?

11. What are the benefits of having hearts filled with gratitude?

LIFE LESSONS

Imitating God can affect many areas of life. The standards of love, light, and wisdom that describe part of God's holy and perfect character are not characteristics we can duplicate exactly, but only imitate. As humans, we bear the image of God; as believers in Jesus, we seek to live up to his pattern. He has invited us to live that way and has promised us the help we will need to live that way. Progress will show an increasing presence of love, light, and wisdom in our lives.

DEVOTION

God, you've given us such a great promise, the promise of salvation. Forgive us, Father, when we sometimes put more hope in the things of this earth than in the incredible promises of your heaven. Teach us to live in your light.

For more Bible passages on living in the light, see John 3:19–21; Acts 26:15–18; Romans 13:11–14; 2 Corinthians 4:6; 1 Peter 2:9–10.

To complete the book of Ephesians during this twelve-part study, read Ephesians 5:1–20.

JOURNALING

Why do I sometimes choose darkness instead of light?

DON'T MISS THE YIELD SIGNS

MAX LUCADO

REFLECTION

Most of us can think of a situation where we have laughed in spite of ourselves. Things got so ridiculously chaotic that there was nothing left to do but laugh and bear it! Describe a time when you wanted to be mad, but somehow laughter broke through instead. Think of other occasions when you may have stumbled into a better response than you would have if you were reacting as normal.

SITUATION

With this passage Paul reaches the heart of his practical theology. He focuses briefly on three crucial relationships that will test our understanding of cooperation with one another and obedience to God: marriage, family, and work relations.

OBSERVATION

Read Ephesians 5:21–33 from the NCV or the NKJV.

NCV

21 *Yield to obey each other because you respect Christ.*

22 *Wives, yield to your husbands, as you do to the Lord,* 23 *because the husband is the head of the wife, as Christ is the head of the church. And he is the Savior of the body, which is the church.* 24 *As the church yields to Christ, so you wives should yield to your husbands in everything.*

25 *Husbands, love your wives as Christ loved the church and gave himself for it* 26 *to make it belong to God. Christ used the word to make the church clean by washing it with water.* 27 *He died so that he could give the church to himself like a bride in all her beauty. He died so that the church could be pure and without fault, with no evil or sin or any other wrong thing in it.* 28 *In the same way, husbands should love their wives as they love their own bodies. The man who loves his wife loves himself.* 29 *No one ever hates his own body, but feeds and takes care of it. And that is what Christ does for the church,* 30 *because we are parts of his body.* 31 *The Scripture says, "So a man will leave his father and mother and be united with his wife, and the two will become one body."* 32 *That secret is very important—I am talking about Christ and the church.* 33 *But each one of you must love his wife as he loves himself, and a wife must respect her husband.*

NKJV

21 *Submitting to one another in the fear of God.*

22 *Wives, submit to your own husbands, as to the Lord.* 23 *For the husband is head of the wife, as also Christ is head of the church; and He is the Savior of the body.* 24 *Therefore, just as the church is subject to Christ, so let the wives be to their own husbands in everything.*

25 *Husbands, love your wives, just as Christ also loved the church and gave Himself for her,* 26 *that He might sanctify and cleanse her with the washing of water by the word,* 27 *that He might present her to Himself a glorious church, not having spot or wrinkle or any such thing, but that she should be holy and without blemish.* 28 *So husbands ought to love their own wives as their own bodies; he who loves his wife loves himself.* 29 *For no one ever hated his own flesh, but nourishes and cherishes it, just as the Lord does the church.* 30 *For we are members of His body, of His flesh and of His bones.* 31 *"For this reason a man shall leave his father and mother and be joined to his wife, and the two shall become one flesh."* 32 *This is a great mystery, but I speak concerning Christ and the church.* 33 *Nevertheless let each one of you in particular so love his own wife as himself, and let the wife see that she respects her husband.*

EXPLORATION

1. What makes it difficult to yield to someone else's wants and needs instead of your own? Is the term *submission* an absolutely negative term? When might it be positive?

2. This passage compares the husband's role in a marriage to Christ's role as the head of the church. What responsibilities, then, does the husband have?

3. How can wives honor their husbands as the church honors Christ?

4. In what ways can husbands give their lives for their wives as this passage says they should?

5. What is the relationship between love and respect in a marriage?

INSPIRATION

You came home cranky because a deadline got moved up. She came home grumpy because the day-care forgot to give your five-year-old her throat medicine. Each of you wanted a little sympathy from the other, but neither got any. So there you sit at the dinner table—cranky and grumpy—with little Emily. Emily folds her hands to pray (as she has been taught), and the two of you bow your heads (but not your hearts) and listen. From where this prayer comes, God only knows.

"God, it's Emily. How are you? I'm fine, thank you. Mom and Dad are mad. I don't know why. We've got birds and toys and mashed potatoes and each other. Maybe you can get them to stop being mad? Please do, or it's just gonna be you and me having any fun tonight. Amen."

The prayer is answered before it's finished, you both look up in the middle and laugh at the end and shake your heads and say you're sorry. And you both thank God for the little voice who reminded you about what matters.

That's what "lovebursts" do . . . Lovebursts. Spontaneous affection. Tender moments of radiant love. Ignited devotion. Explosions of tenderness . . . They remind you about what matters. A telegram delivered to the back door of the familiar, telling you to treasure the treasure you've got while you've got it. A whisper from an angel, or someone who sounds like one, reminding you that what you have is greater than what you want and that what is urgent is not always what matters. (From *He Still Moves Stones* by Max Lucado)

REACTION

6. When both the husband and wife need the other's sympathy or attention at the same time, how can both get their needs met?

7. List some tactics that help a couple regain perspective when circumstances get tense.

8. Name some issues or circumstances that seem urgent but don't really matter in the long run.

9. What does it mean to "yield" or "submit" to someone or something?

10. In what ways is the church like a bride? (See Revelation 21:1–5.)

11. In what ways will respecting Christ help couples yield to each other?

LIFE LESSONS

Because a long-term relationship involves two people, it cannot be a democracy. Life presents decisions that must be made even if there is a disagreement. In a union of two, there can be harmony on most issues. But when there is a non-negotiable disagreement, someone must have the responsibility of the deciding vote. This responsibility must be stated beforehand and affirmed in the middle of the situation. This is the essential challenge and opportunity of love and respect.

The lessons God teaches are not just learned. They are learned, lived, and then learned again and again. And all the while, living goes on.

DEVOTION

God, give us strength as we try to be more like Jesus in our homes. Keep the evil one away from us. Keep us close to you. Let our homes be testimonies of your love for us. When people look inside, let them see how you have loved the world.

For more Bible passages on loving marriages, see Colossians 3:18–19; Hebrews 13:4; 1 Peter 3:1–7.

To complete the book of Ephesians during this twelve-part study, read Ephesians 5:21–33.

JOURNALING

In what ways can I bend more this week to mend a relationship?

BEING GOOD PARENTS, BEING GOOD BOSSES

MAX LUCADO

REFLECTION

What is one of your strongest memories of your mom and/or dad? Describe some of the ways you have consciously tried to be like them.

SITUATION

Paul lived in a time and culture in which women had few rights. Children and slaves had practically no rights at all. Wives, children, and slaves were often treated as little more than property. When Paul addressed these persons as individuals capable of privileges, responsibilities, and expectations, he was significantly elevating their status in society. He gave them worth by addressing them. He gave them importance by requiring others to treat them with respect.

OBSERVATION

Read Ephesians 6:1–9 from the NCV or the NKJV.

NCV

¹Children, obey your parents as the Lord wants, because this is the right thing to do. ²The command says, "Honor your father and mother." This is the first command that has a promise with it—³"Then everything will be well with you, and you will have a long life on the earth."

⁴Fathers, do not make your children angry, but raise them with the training and teaching of the Lord.

⁵Slaves, obey your masters here on earth with fear and respect and from a sincere heart, just as you obey Christ. ⁶You must do this not only while they are watching you, to please them. With all your heart you must do what God wants as people who are obeying Christ. ⁷Do your work with enthusiasm. Work as if you were serving the Lord, not as if you were serving only men and women. ⁸Remember that the Lord will give a reward to everyone, slave or free, for doing good.

⁹Masters, in the same way, be good to your slaves. Do not threaten them. Remember that the One who is your Master and their Master is in heaven, and he treats everyone alike.

NKJV

¹Children, obey your parents in the Lord, for this is right. ²"Honor your father and mother," which is the first commandment with promise: ³"that it may be well with you and you may live long on the earth."

⁴And you, fathers, do not provoke your children to wrath, but bring them up in the training and admonition of the Lord.

⁵Bondservants, be obedient to those who are your masters according to the flesh, with fear and trembling, in sincerity of heart, as to Christ; ⁶not with eyeservice, as men-pleasers, but as bondservants of Christ, doing the will of God from the heart, ⁷with goodwill doing service, as to the Lord, and not to men, ⁸knowing that whatever good anyone does, he will receive the same from the Lord, whether he is a slave or free.

⁹And you, masters, do the same things to them, giving up threatening, knowing that your own Master also is in heaven, and there is no partiality with Him.

EXPLORATION

1. God's standard for children is that they obey their parents as God wants them to. Describe that kind of obedience.

2. How can dads keep from making their children angry? How does this relate to the fact that kids often get upset when they are corrected or disciplined?

3. In what ways do Paul's instructions to slaves (to work with integrity whether the master is watching or not) apply to employees?

4. Paul reminds masters that they and their slaves are both serving the same master (God). In what ways does this truth apply to bosses or managers?

5. Why would the Bible command us to do our work with enthusiasm?

INSPIRATION

What does it mean to honor your parents? We can see what it means if we will look at the word *honor* in the Scriptures. In Hebrew, the word for "honor" is *kabed*. This word literally means, "to be heavy, weighty, to honor." Even today, we still link the idea of being heavy with honoring a person.

When the President of the United States or some other important person speaks, people often say that his words "carry a lot of weight." Someone whose words are weighty is someone worthy of honor and respect. However, we can learn even more about what it means to honor someone by looking at its opposite in Scriptures . . .

The literal meaning of the word "curse" (*qalal*) was "to make light, of little weight, to dishonor." If we go back to our example above, if we dishonor a person we would say, "Their words carry little weight." The contrast is striking!

When Paul tells us to honor our parents, he is telling us that they are worthy of high value and respect. In modern-day terms, we could call them a heavyweight in our lives! Just the opposite is true if we choose to dishonor our parents.

Some people treat their parents as if they are a layer of dust on a table. Dust weighs almost nothing and can be swept away with a brush of the hand. Dust is a nuisance and an eyesore that clouds any real beauty the table might have. Paul tells us that such an attitude should not be a part of how any child views his or her parents and for good reason. If we fail to honor our parents, we not only do what is wrong and dishonor God, but we also literally drain ourselves of life! (From *The Gift of the Blessing* by Gary Smalley and John Trent)

REACTION

6. In what ways can we honor our parents? We usually concentrate on what it means for children to honor their parents when the children are still quite young. But it's equally important to consider what this means as we get older. What does it mean to honor your parents as a college student? Or as a newly married couple?

7. What makes honoring our parents difficult?

8. Is disregarding our parents the same as dishonoring them? Why or why not?

9. In what way is God honored by our diligent work in our jobs?

10. How do you think God will reward everyone for doing good?

11. List some ways employers threaten employees in today's world.

LIFE LESSONS

The challenge in relationships comes in part because they are two-sided arrangements. This passage looks at both sides—children and parents, workers and bosses. Spiritual maturity comes when we can see the side other than our own. A sense of our needs, desires, and rights comes naturally; an appreciation for others' needs, desires, and rights comes not-so-naturally. And beyond, the willingness to act on what we understand of someone else's position depends heavily on God's help.

DEVOTION

Lift up our eyes, Father, that we might see ourselves and those around us as you see us. Help us respond to one another with love and compassion. Help us to be like you.

For more Bible passages on parents and children, see Deuteronomy 6:6–9; Proverbs 1:8; 6:20; 22:6; Colossians 3:20; 1 Timothy 3:2–5; Titus 2:3–5.

To complete the book of Ephesians during this twelve-part study, read Ephesians 6:1–9.

LIFE LESSONS WITH MAX LUCADO

JOURNALING

What can I do to honor my parents or the memory of my parents this week?

L E S S O N   T W E L V E

BE A
WINNER!

MAX
LUCADO

REFLECTION

Think of a time when you were involved in a victory of some kind. What are the feelings that come from being on the winning side?

SITUATION

In closing, Paul reminded his readers that a very real battle was waging against a very real enemy. He wanted to equip them for a life of adventure in God's service. Reciting a list of spiritual resources, he spelled out the armor God has issued to all believers in Christ.

OBSERVATION

Read Ephesians 6:10–20 from the NCV or the NKJV.

NCV

¹⁰Finally, be strong in the Lord and in his great power. ¹¹Put on the full armor of God so that you can fight against the devil's evil tricks. ¹²Our fight is not against people on earth but against the rulers and authorities and the powers of this world's darkness, against the spiritual powers of evil in the heavenly world. ¹³That is why you need to put on God's full armor. Then on the day of evil you will be able to stand strong. And when you have finished the whole fight, you will still be standing. ¹⁴So stand strong, with the belt of truth tied around your waist and the protection of right living on your chest. ¹⁵On your feet wear the Good News of peace to help you stand strong. ¹⁶And also use the shield of faith with which you can stop all the burning arrows of the Evil One. ¹⁷Accept God's salvation as your helmet, and take the sword of the Spirit, which is the word of God. ¹⁸Pray in the Spirit at all times with all kinds of prayers, asking for everything you need. To do this you must always be ready and never give up. Always pray for all God's people.

¹⁹Also pray for me that when I speak, God will give me words so that I can tell the secret of the Good News without fear. ²⁰I have been sent to preach this Good News, and I am doing that now, here in prison. Pray that when I preach the Good News I will speak without fear, as I should.

NKJV

¹⁰Finally, my brethren, be strong in the Lord and in the power of His might. ¹¹Put on the whole armor of God, that you may be able to stand against the wiles of the devil. ¹²For we do not wrestle against flesh and blood, but against principalities, against powers, against the rulers of the darkness of this age, against spiritual hosts of wickedness in the heavenly places. ¹³Therefore take up the whole armor of God, that you may be able to withstand in the evil day, and having done all, to stand.

¹⁴Stand therefore, having girded your waist with truth, having put on the breastplate of righteousness, ¹⁵and having shod your feet with the preparation of the gospel of peace; ¹⁶above all, taking the shield of faith with which you will be able to quench all the fiery darts of the wicked one. ¹⁷And take the helmet of salvation, and the sword of the Spirit, which is the word of God; ¹⁸praying always with all prayer and supplication in the Spirit, being watchful to this end with all perseverance and supplication for all the saints—¹⁹and for me, that utterance may be given to me, that I may open my mouth boldly to make known the mystery of the gospel, ²⁰for which I am an ambassador in chains; that in it I may speak boldly, as I ought to speak.

EXPLORATION

1. What is the purpose of a soldier's armor? Even today, terms like *body armor* continue in the vocabulary of warriors.

2. List some of the devil's "tricks" that this passage might be referring to (v. 11 NCV).

3. In what ways does "right living" protect us?

4. Why do you think the gospel was compared to footwear?

5. List some ways a life of prayer will benefit us in spiritual warfare.

INSPIRATION

Triumph is a precious thing. We honor the triumphant. The gallant soldier sitting astride his steed. The determined explorer returning from his discovery. The winning athlete holding aloft the triumphant trophy of victory. Yes, we love triumph.

Triumph brings with it a swell of purpose and meaning. When I'm triumphant, I'm worthy. When I'm triumphant, I count. When I'm triumphant, I'm significant.

Triumph is fleeting, though. Hardly does one taste victory before it is gone; achieved, yet now history. No one remains champion forever. Time for yet another conquest, another victory. Perhaps this is the absurdity of Paul's claim: "But thanks be to God, who always leads us in triumphal procession in Christ" (2 Cor. 2:14 NIV).

The triumph of Christ is not temporary. "Triumphant in Christ" is not an event or an occasion. It's not fleeting. To be triumphant in Christ is a life-style . . . a state of being! To triumph in Christ is not something we do, it's something we are.

Here is the big difference between victory in Christ and victory in the world: A victor in the world rejoices over something he did—swimming the English Channel, climbing Mt. Everest, making a million. But the believer rejoices over who he is: a child of God, a forgiven sinner, an heir of eternity. As the hymn goes, "heir of salvation, purchase of God, born of his Spirit, washed in his blood."

Nothing can separate us from our triumph in Christ. Nothing! Our triumph is not based upon our feelings but upon God's gift. Our triumph is based not upon our perfection but upon God's forgiveness. How precious is this triumph! For even though we are pressed on every side, the victory is still ours. Nothing can alter the loyalty of God.

A friend of mine recently lost his father to death. The faith of his father had for years served as an inspiration for many. In moments alone with the body of his father, my friend said this thought kept coming to his mind as he looked at his daddy's face: "You won. You won. You won!" As Joan of Arc said when she was abandoned by those who should have stood by her, "It is better to be alone with God. His friendship will not fail me, nor his counsel, nor his love. In his strength I will dare and dare and dare until I die."

"Triumphant in Christ." It is not something we do. It's something we are. (From *Shaped by God* by Max Lucado)

REACTION

6. In what ways are Christians like soldiers?

7. Define spiritual victory.

8. How does the armor described in Ephesians equip us for our battles? What degree of battle readiness would you give yourself?

9. In what way is faith like a shield?

10. How is salvation like a helmet?

11. In what way is the Word of God like a sword? What would it take for you to feel comfortable going into battle with this "sword"?

LIFE LESSONS

God does all the crucial work and provides all the essential resources. He challenges and encourages us to use them. Each item of spiritual armor listed in this passage comes to us as a gift from God. He guarantees their effectiveness. But their effectiveness is limited in our lives by our willingness to "put them on" and use them. Along with walking by faith, walking worthy, walking in light, walking in love, there are also times for standing firm. Life situations may involve taking a stand, and when we do, it's best not to do so unarmed. With faith, truth, salvation, the Word of God, and prayer, God has promised us victory.

DEVOTION

We give you praise. We honor and glorify your name. You truly are the King of kings and the Lord of lords. We thank you and worship you and will follow you forever and ever. Amen.

For more Bible passages on victory in Christ, see Psalm 44:4–8; 60:12; 118:13–16; Proverbs 2:6–8; 21:30–31; 1 Corinthians 15:54–57; 1 John 5:3–5.

To complete the book of Ephesians during this twelve-part study, read Ephesians 6:10–23.